MACMILLAN McGRAW-HILL
Science

Lucy H. Daniel
Jay Hackett
Richard H. Moyer
JoAnne Vasquez

About the Cover

Canadian lynx live in forest areas. They are good climbers and can swim well in rivers and streams. They have padded feet that are like snowshoes. These help the lynx walk on top of the snow.

INQUIRY **What else would you like to know about Canadian lynx? Write your own question or questions to answer.**

Mc Graw Hill **Macmillan McGraw-Hill**

Program Authors

Dr. Lucy H. Daniel
Teacher, Consultant
Rutherford County Schools, North Carolina

Dr. Jay Hackett
Professor Emeritus of Earth Sciences
University of Northern Colorado

Dr. Richard H. Moyer
Professor of Science Education
University of Michigan-Dearborn

Dr. JoAnne Vasquez
Elementary Science Education Consultant
Mesa Public Schools, Arizona
NSTA Past President

Contributing Authors

Lucille Villegas Barrera, M.Ed.
Elementary Science Supervisor
Houston Independent School District
Houston, Texas

Mulugheta Teferi, M.A.
St. Louis Public Schools
St. Louis, Missouri

Dinah Zike, M.Ed.
Dinah Might Adventures LP
San Antonio, Texas

The features in this textbook entitled "Amazing Stories," as well as the unit openers, were developed in collaboration with the National Geographic Society's School Publishing Division.

RFB&D ⓥ
learning through listening

Students with print disabilities may be eligible to obtain an accessible, audio version of the pupil edition of this textbook. Please call Recording for the Blind & Dyslexic at 1-800-221-4792 for complete information.

The McGraw·Hill Companies

Published by Macmillan/McGraw-Hill, of McGraw-Hill Education, a division of The McGraw-Hill Companies, Inc., Two Penn Plaza, New York, New York 10121.

Printed in the United States of America
ISBN 0-02-282586-X/2

3 4 5 6 7 8 9 027/043 09 08 07 06 05

Life Science

Consultants

Dr. Carol Baskin
University of Kentucky
Lexington, KY

Dr. Joe W. Crim
University of Georgia
Athens, GA

Dr. Marie DiBerardino
Allegheny University of
Health Sciences
Philadelphia, PA

Dr. R. E. Duhrkopf
Baylor University
Waco, TX

Dr. Dennis L. Nelson
Montana State University
Bozeman, MT

Dr. Fred Sack
Ohio State University
Columbus, OH

Dr. Martin VanDyke
Denver, CO

Dr. E. Peter Volpe
Mercer University
Macon, GA

Earth Science

Consultants

Dr. Clarke Alexander
Skidaway Institute of
Oceanography
Savannah, GA

Dr. Suellen Cabe
Pembroke State University
Pembroke, NC

Dr. Thomas A. Davies
Texas A & M University
College Station, TX

Dr. Ed Geary
Geological Society of America
Boulder, CO

Dr. David C. Kopaska-Merkel
Geological Survey of Alabama
Tuscaloosa, AL

Physical Science

Consultants

Dr. Bonnie Buratti
Jet Propulsion Lab
Pasadena, CA

Dr. Shawn Carlson
Society of Amateur Scientists
San Diego, CA

Dr. Karen Kwitter
Williams College
Williamstown, MA

Dr. Steven Souza
Williamstown, MA

Dr. Joseph P. Straley
University of Kentucky
Lexington, KY

Dr. Thomas Troland
University of Kentucky
Lexington, KY

Dr. Josephine Davis Wallace
University of North Carolina
Charlotte, NC

Consultant for Primary Grades

Donna Harrell Lubcker
East Texas Baptist University
Marshall, TX

Teacher Reviewers (continued)

Beth Lewis
Wilmington, North Carolina

Cindy Hatchell
Wilmington, North Carolina

Cindy Kahler
Carrboro, North Carolina

Diane Leusky
Chapel Hill, North Carolina

Heather Sutton
Wilmington, North Carolina

Crystal Stephens
Valdese, North Carolina

Meg Millard
Chapel Hill, North Carolina

Patricia Underwood
Randleman, North Carolina

E. Joy Mermin
Chapel Hill, North Carolina

Yolanda Evans
Wilmington, North Carolina

Tim Gilbride
Pennsauken, New Jersey

Helene Reifowitz
Nesconsit, New York

Tina Craig
Tulsa, Oklahoma

Deborah Harwell
Lawton, Oklahoma

Kathleen Conn
West Chester, Pennsylvania

Heath Renninger Zerbe
Tremont, Pennsylvania

Patricia Armillei
Holland, Pennsylvania

Sue Workman
Cedar City, Utah

Peg Jensen
Hartford, Wisconsin

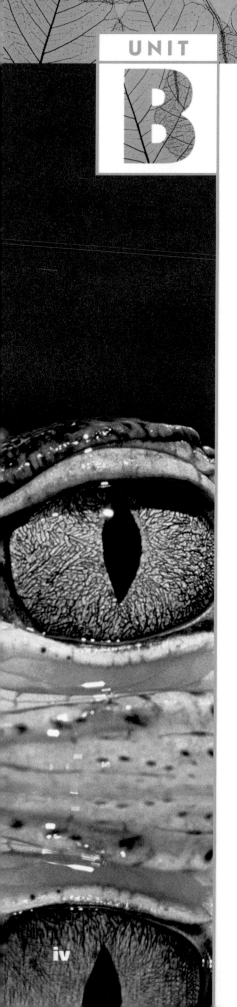

Life Science

UNIT B

Homes for Plants and Animals PAGE B1

UNIT B

Homes for Plants and Animals

LOOK!

What is this animal?
Where does it live?
Take a good look!

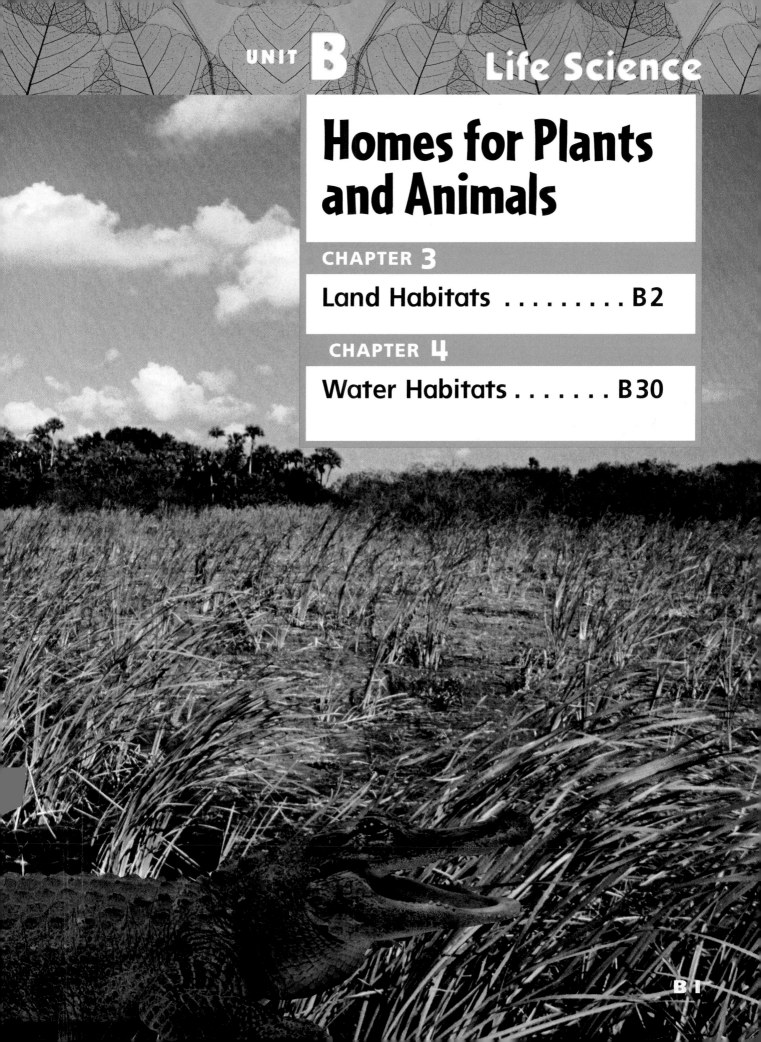

Homes for Plants and Animals

Land Habitats

Vocabulary

habitat, B6

woodland
   forest, B10

migrate, B13

rain forest, B16

desert, B20

Arctic, B24

Did You Ever Wonder?

Why do prairie dogs pop up out of holes? They live below the ground. When a prairie dog sees danger, it barks and hides in the ground.

INQUIRY SKILL **Communicate** how a cat acts when it sees danger. Tell how you know.

Where Plants and Animals Live

Get Ready

Living in the mountains is not easy! The weather is cold. The ground is rocky. How does this mountain goat get what it needs to live?

Inquiry Skill

You **communicate** when you talk, write, or draw to share your ideas.

Explore Activity

Where do animals live?

paper

crayons

What to do

1 Look at the footprints. What animal do you think made them?

2 How does the shape of the feet help this animal? **Communicate** your idea with a partner.

3 Draw a picture of the animal. Show where it lives.

4 FURTHER INQUIRY **Communicate** what it needs to live. How does it get food and water?

What is a habitat?

A **habitat** is a place where plants and animals meet their needs. Different plants and animals live in different habitats.

The animals in these pictures live near water. This is where they can find what they need to live.

water strider

otter

The animals in a habitat need plants. They also need each other. Some animals use plants for shelter. Many eat plants. Some animals eat other animals. This bird lives near water because it eats the fish that live there.

▷ **How is the kingfisher meeting its needs?**

kingfisher

Think and Write

1. What is a habitat?

2. What do animals get from their habitats?

HOME ACTIVITY Take a walk with a family member. Look for plants and animals in a habitat.

catfish

Life in a Woodland Forest

Get Ready

A place with many trees is a good habitat for a chipmunk. How could you show where a chipmunk lives?

Inquiry Skill

You **make a model** when you make something to show a place or a thing.

Explore Activity

What is a forest like?

What to do

1 **Make a model** of a forest. Place the soil, plant, and rocks in a bottle.

2 Water the soil. Add the pill bug. Cover the bottle with plastic wrap. Poke holes in it. Place it near a window.

3 Observe your model. Record how it changes.

4 FURTHER INQUIRY **Make a model** of the forest in winter. Draw a picture to show how it would change.

What you need

bottle

soil

plant

plastic wrap

rocks

plastic spoon

pill bug

What lives in a woodland forest?

A **woodland forest** is a habitat that gets enough rain and sunlight for trees to grow well. Some animals may use the trees for food. Some eat nuts and insects found on trees.

mushrooms

raccoon

A tree can be a home for many living things. Plants may grow on the outside of the tree. Small animals may make their homes inside the tree.

Some animals may use other animals for shelter. A small insect may live on a bigger animal's body.

▷ What are some animals that live in this woodland forest?

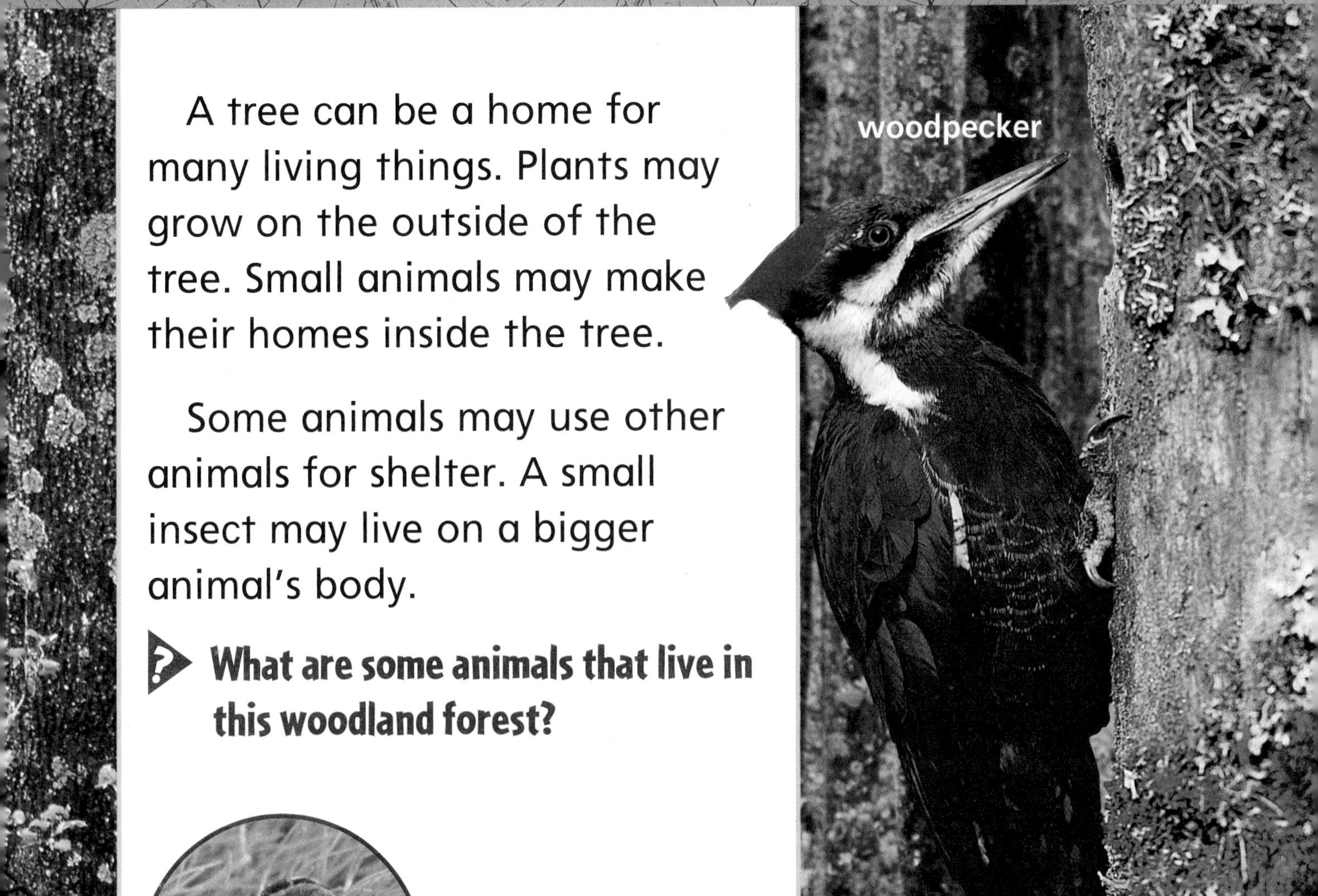

woodpecker

insect living on a deer

foxes

How does a woodland forest change?

A woodland forest has four seasons. In spring many forest animals have their young. Leaves begin to grow on trees.

spring

deer

In summer woodland forests are warm. Leaves on the trees are green. Animals can find a lot of food to eat.

deer mouse

summer

In fall the weather gets cool. The leaves on many trees change color and fall to the ground. Sometimes plant seeds stick to animals. Animals move them to new places where they may grow.

fall

bison

Some forest animals store food for the winter. Many birds **migrate**, or move to warmer places.

chipmunk

In winter many trees have no leaves. It is cold and food is harder to find. Some animals go into a deep sleep.

▷ **How do the trees in a woodland forest change during fall and winter?**

Think and Write

1. What is a woodland forest?

2. How do animals help the plants of a woodland forest?

HOME ACTIVITY Make a book of seasons. Draw a picture of what you do in each season.

winter

Life in a Rain Forest

Get Ready

These fuzzy creatures are leaf bats. They live in a habitat called a rain forest. How are they using the leaf to meet their needs?

Inquiry Skill

You **infer** when you use what you know to figure something out.

Explore Activity

How can a rain forest animal find shelter?

What to do

1 Fold a paper plate in half. Glue five cotton balls inside the fold.

2 Stand up the plate like a tent. Put it in the tray. Pour a little water over the paper plate.

3 Observe the cotton balls.

4 FURTHER INQUIRY **Infer** why leaf bats find shelter inside rain forest leaves.

What you need

paper plate

cotton balls

glue

aluminum tray

water

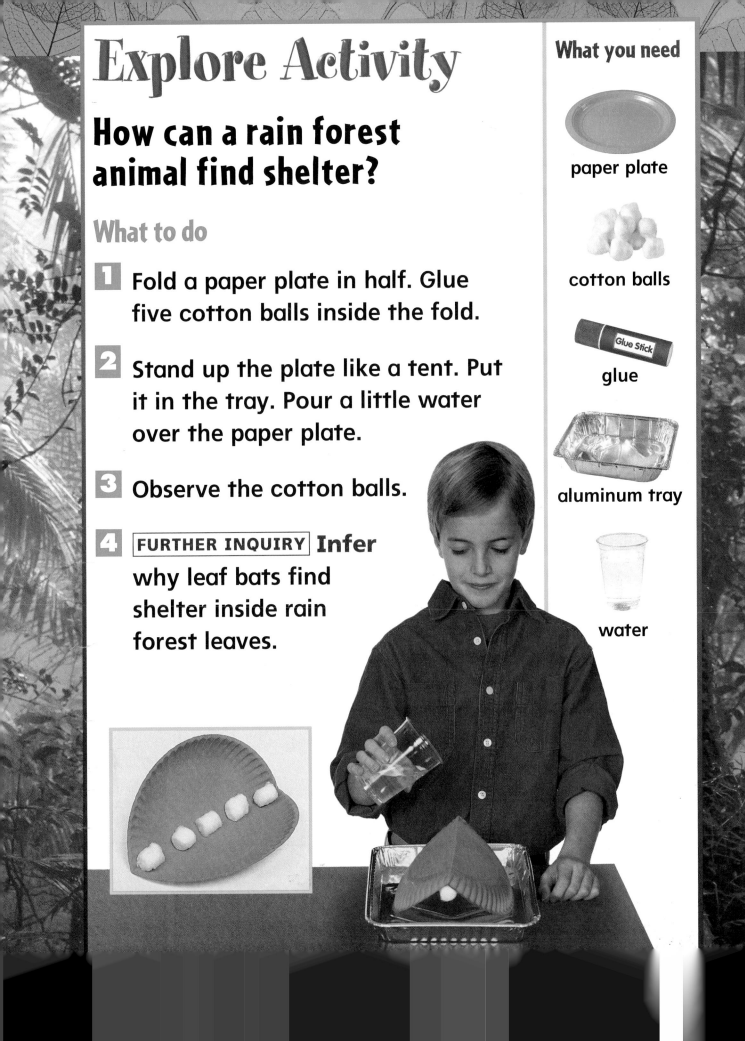

What lives in a rain forest?

A **rain forest** is a habitat where it rains almost every day. It is warm in many rain forests. There can be more than 70 inches of rain each year. Because there is a lot of rain, many trees and plants grow well. The trees and plants are food and shelter for many animals.

A tree frog finds water.

An ocelot hunts for food.

There are many tall trees in a rain forest. The tops of the trees get a lot of sunlight. Less sunlight reaches the rain forest floor.

Monkeys and parrots are two kinds of animals that live in the tops of trees. They eat the leaves, fruits, and nuts that grow there.

parrot

monkey

> **How do these rain forest animals get what they need?**

Think and Write

1. Describe a rain forest.

2. How do some rain forest animals use plants?

MORE TO READ

Read **Nature's Green Umbrella: Tropical Rain Forests** by Gail Gibbons.

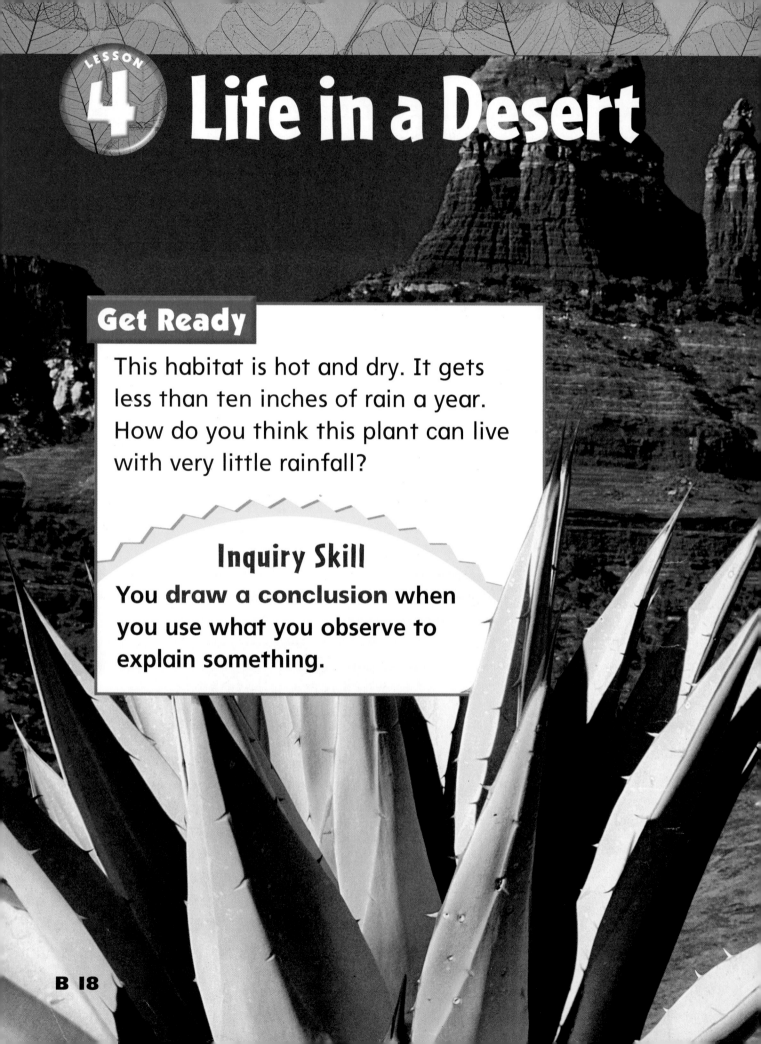

Life in a Desert

Get Ready

This habitat is hot and dry. It gets less than ten inches of rain a year. How do you think this plant can live with very little rainfall?

Inquiry Skill

You **draw a conclusion** when you use what you observe to explain something.

Explore Activity

How does the shape of a leaf help a plant?

paper towels

scissors

water

plastic wrap

What to do

1 Cut two leaf shapes from the paper towels. Roll up one leaf.

> **BE CAREFUL!** Scissors are sharp!

2 Place both leaf shapes on plastic wrap. Wet them both.

3 Check both leaf shapes every 15 minutes. Which leaf shape stayed wet longer?

4 FURTHER INQUIRY

Draw a **conclusion** about which kind of leaf you might find in a dry place.

What lives in a desert?

A **desert** is a dry habitat. It gets less rain in a year than most plants and animals need to live.

Some desert plants, such as a cactus, can live a long time without rain. They store water in their thick stems.

Some desert animals get the water they need from their food.

jackrabbit

cactus

rattlesnake

lizard

Some deserts are very hot during the day. Many animals hide below ground or under rocks to keep cool. At night they come out to look for food.

▷ **What are some animals that live in the desert?**

Think and Write

1. What is a desert?

2. How do some desert animals keep cool when the sun is hot?

LOG ON Visit www.science.mmhschool.com to learn more about deserts.

Life in the Arctic

Arctic fox in summer

Get Ready

This Arctic fox had a dark coat last summer. Then its coat turned white in winter. What color coat do you think the fox will have next summer? Tell why.

Inquiry Skill

You **predict** when you use what you know to tell what you think will happen.

Arctic fox in winter

Explore Activity

How can color help animals hide?

What to do

1 Fold the white paper. Spread out the circles on one half of the paper. Fold over the other side.

2 Your partner will uncover the circles and count to ten. Pick up as many circles as you can.

3 How many circles of each color did you pick up? How does color make it easier or harder to pick up the circles?

4 FURTHER INQUIRY
Predict what will happen if you use brown paper. Then try it.

white paper

20 white circles

20 brown circles

What lives in the Arctic?

The **Arctic** is a very cold place near the North Pole. Snow is on the ground for much of the year. It melts for only a short time in the summer.

Arctic plants

In summer plants can grow. They grow very low to the ground. This helps them stay safe from strong winds. Many animals eat these plants.

musk ox

caribou

Arctic terns

In winter most plants die. Animals that eat plants migrate, or move, to warmer places to find food.

Some animals have white winter coats to blend in with the snow. This helps keep them safe. Polar bears make snow dens. Safe in the dens, the female bears can give birth to their cubs.

▷ **How do these living things meet their needs?**

polar bears

Think and Write

1. When do most plants grow in the Arctic?

2. Why do some animals leave the Arctic in the winter?

 **MORE TO READ** Read **Crinkleroot's Guide to Knowing Animal Habitats** by Jim Arnosky.

What is your habitat like?

You have learned about different habitats. You live in a habitat, too. Observe the plants and animals that live near you.

Try This!

Writing that Compares Look at these pictures. Compare the habitat where you live with one of these habitats. Write how the habitats are alike. Then write how they are different.

In the Rain Forest

It rains almost every day in the rain forest. The raindrops in the graph show how many inches of rain fall in April, May, and June.

Rain Forest Rain Fall

April	💧	💧	💧	💧	💧
May	💧	💧	💧		
June	💧	💧	💧	💧	

Try This!

Use the graph. Compare the amounts of rainfall. Did more rain fall during May or June? Tell how you know.

Vocabulary

Arctic, B24

desert, B20

habitat, B6

migrate, B13

rain forest, B16

woodland forest, B10

Use each word once for items 1–6.

1 A place where plants and animals find what they need to live is a ____ .

2 A habitat where very little rain falls is called a ____ .

3 Animals ____ when they move to warmer places in winter.

4 A habitat where many trees grow and seasons change is called a ____ .

5 A habitat that gets rain almost every day is a ____ .

6 Snow is on the ground for much of the year in the ____ .

Science Ideas

7 The Mojave Desert gets 5 inches of rain a year. Death Valley gets 2 inches of rain a year. How much more rain does the Mojave Desert get? Write a number sentence to solve.

8 Which of these animals does not live in a desert? Where does it live? How do you know?

rattlesnake

chipmunk

lizard

Inquiry Skill: Communicate

9 How does this animal's color help it stay safe? Write about it.

READ
A Science Project for George
by Jennifer Jacobson
Now You See It, Now You Don't
by Geof Smith

Did You Ever Wonder? | INQUIRY SKILL | What kind of sounds do animals make? **Draw a conclusion** about why animals make them.

Water Habitats

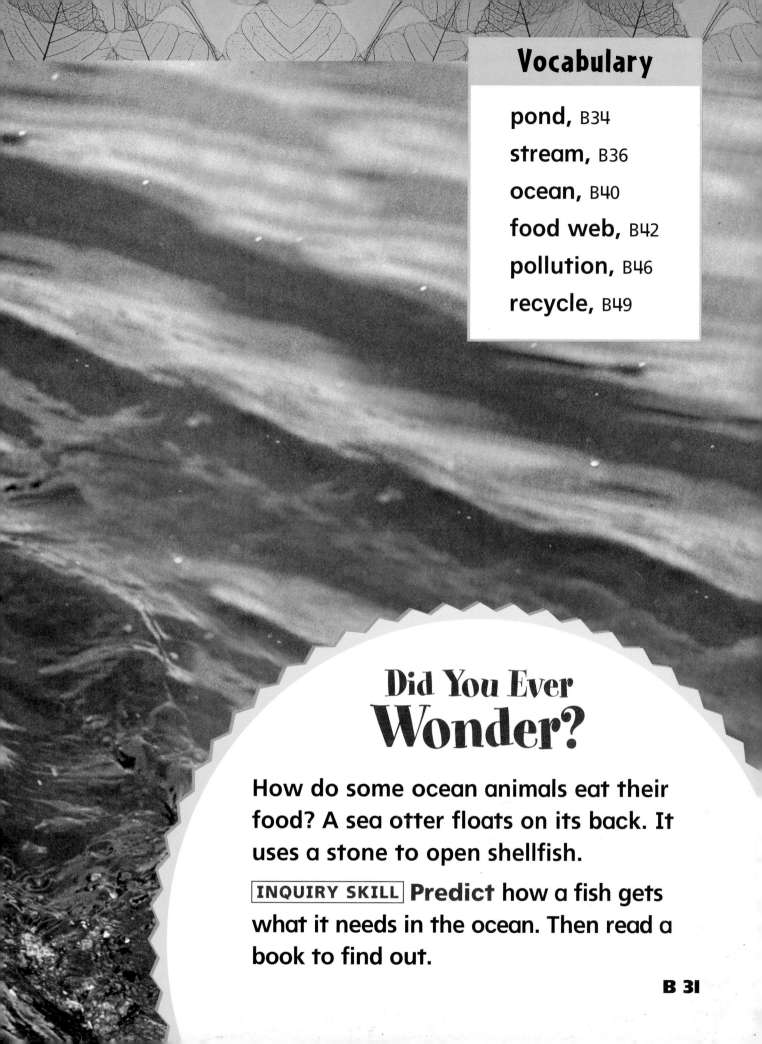

Did You Ever Wonder?

How do some ocean animals eat their food? A sea otter floats on its back. It uses a stone to open shellfish.

INQUIRY SKILL **Predict** how a fish gets what it needs in the ocean. Then read a book to find out.

Life in a Fresh Water Habitat

Get Ready

These ducks live in a pond. They spend much of their day in the water. How do you think ducks are able to stay dry?

Inquiry Skill

You **infer** when you use what you know to figure something out.

Explore Activity

How does a duck stay dry?

What to do

paper

scissors

1 Draw and cut out two ducks.

> **BE CAREFUL!** Scissors are sharp!

crayons

2 Use a crayon to color both sides of one duck. Press hard. Make sure to color all of it. Do not color the second duck.

3 Drip water on one side of each paper duck. Use a spoon. Which one stayed drier? Why?

cup of water

spoon

4 **FURTHER INQUIRY** **Infer** how a duck's feathers help it stay dry.

cattails

What lives in a pond?

A **pond** is a fresh water habitat.
Fresh water has little or no salt in it.
Like water in a pool, pond water
stays in one place. Plants grow in
and around the pond. Some plants
even float on the water.

bullfrog on
water lily

Many pond fish eat water plants
and insects. Birds make nests with
pond grass. Beavers build homes
with branches from nearby trees.

beaver

A pond can change through the year. Some ponds freeze in the winter. Fish swim below the ice. Turtles and frogs dig into the mud for warmth. Some insects sleep in the soil near the pond.

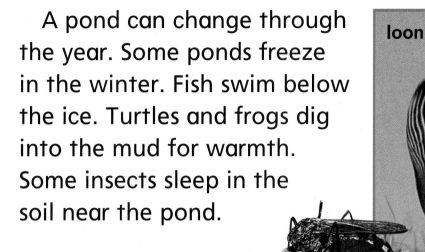
mosquito

loon

In summer a pond may dry up if there is not enough rain. Some pond animals leave and find new homes.

▷ **How do these animals get what they need in a pond habitat?**

perch swimming under ice

What lives in a stream?

A **stream** is a fresh water habitat with moving water. Salmon swim in streams. Sometimes they swim against the flow of the water to find a place to lay eggs.

salmon

otter

Otters find shelter on the sides of streams. Many insects and birds fly above the stream. They dive in the water to find food to eat. Some insects, like dragonflies, begin life in the water. Then they move to land.

gray wagtail

dragonfly

▶ **How do these animals meet their needs?**

Think and Write

1. How are ponds and streams alike? How are they different?

2. What do some pond animals do in the winter?

3. What are some ways animals find food in fresh water habitats?

LOG ON Visit **www.science.mmhschool.com** to learn more about fresh water habitats.

Life in a Salt Water Habitat

Get Ready

Some animals live in a pond. Other animals live in the ocean. What kind of habitat do these two animals live in? How do you know?

Inquiry Skill

You **observe** when you use your senses to learn about the world around you.

Explore Activity

What lives in a salt water habitat?

What to do

1 Fill each container with two cups of water. Add two teaspoons of salt to one container. Mix it.

2 Add $\frac{1}{4}$ teaspoon of brine shrimp eggs to each container.

3 **Observe** what happens every day. Use a hand lens. Can brine shrimp grow in fresh water and salt water? Tell why or why not.

4 **FURTHER INQUIRY** **Observe** how the brine shrimp change.

What you need

brine shrimp eggs

2 clear containers

spoon

salt

measuring spoon

measuring cup

hand lens

What lives in the ocean?

An **ocean** is a large, deep body of salt water. Oceans cover three-fourths of Earth. The salty water can be up to seven miles deep! It is deeper in some places than it is in others.

Most ocean animals and plants need salt water to live. They can not live in fresh water.

dolphin

eel

fish living in coral

Many fish search for sea plants or other fish to eat. Dolphins and whales also swim to find food. They are mammals, so they must come to the surface to breathe air.

Different plants and animals live in different parts of the ocean. Some animals live near the shore. Some live on the ocean floor.

▷ **How are all of these animals alike?**

starfish

lobster

octopus

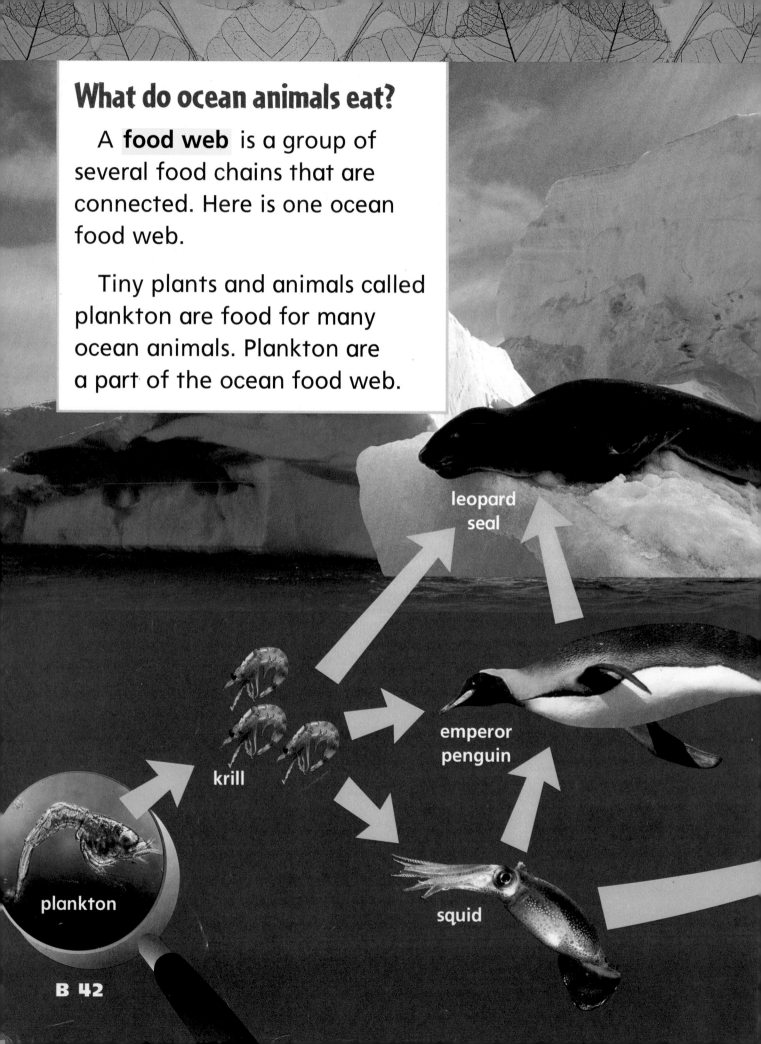

What do ocean animals eat?

A **food web** is a group of several food chains that are connected. Here is one ocean food web.

Tiny plants and animals called plankton are food for many ocean animals. Plankton are a part of the ocean food web.

leopard seal

emperor penguin

krill

plankton

squid

Many fish and krill eat plankton. Larger fish, seals, and penguins eat these fish. Some whales then eat seals and penguins. The arrows in this picture show what is food for each animal.

▶ What does the killer whale eat?

killer whale

Think and Write

1. What is an ocean?

2. How deep can an ocean get in some places?

3. What is a food web?

 **MORE TO READ** Read **The Magic School Bus on the Ocean Floor** by Joanna Cole.

Caring for Earth's Habitats

Get Ready

What if the ocean were covered with black slime? That is what happens when oil spills into the water. What do you think this oil spill will do to the bird and its habitat?

Inquiry Skill

You **predict** when you use what you know to tell what you think will happen.

Explore Activity

What can oil do to a bird's feathers?

tray of water

feather

cup of oil

paper towels

What to do

1 Put the feather in the water. **Predict** what will happen if you pour oil into the water.

2 Pour oil into the water. Tell what happens to the feather.

3 Try to remove the oil. Use paper towels. Is it easy or difficult? Wash your hands.

4 FURTHER INQUIRY **Predict** how oil can make a bird sick. Then read a book to find out.

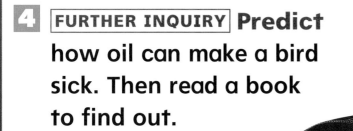

How can we care for the water?

Pollution happens when harmful things are put in water, air, or land. It can hurt living things. We can not make new water, air, or land. That is why we must take care of them.

When there are too many harmful things in water, we can not use it. Animals can get sick. We can help keep water clean by picking up trash. We can tell others about the dangers of pollution. There are also laws against pollution.

▶ **How are these people caring for a water habitat?**

oil spill

Workers help clean up a bird after an oil spill.

How can we care for the air?

Some people burn leaves and trash to get rid of them. This causes air pollution. Cars and factories can cause air pollution, too. There are laws to help keep the air clean. We can help keep the air clean by riding bikes and walking.

▷ **How are these people caring for air?**

air pollution

How can we care for the land?

Every day trees are cut down to clear land for building. Many trees are also cut down for wood and paper. We can help care for the land by planting trees. Tree leaves give off oxygen for us to breathe. Tree roots keep soil from blowing or washing away. Planting trees also makes homes for animals.

planting trees

cleared land

We throw away tons of trash every year. Much of this trash goes to big pits in the ground called landfills. Landfills are getting too full to hold more trash.

landfill

recycling

We can cut down on waste. We can **recycle** paper, glass, cans, and plastic. Recycled waste can be made into new things and used again. People can make shoes, clothes, and toys from recycled plastic.

▷ **How are these people caring for the land?**

Think and Write

1. What is pollution?

2. How does recycling help the garbage problem?

HOME ACTIVITY What can you do to cut down on trash at home?

L·I·N·K

Go Fishing for Facts

Fish come in all shapes and sizes. They live all over the world. Learn about ocean fish. Read *Fishy Facts* by Anne Miranda.

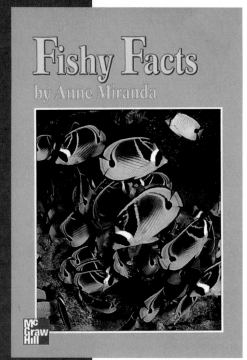

Fishy Facts
by Anne Miranda

Try This!

Use your library to find out more about fish. Pick one fish that you like. Draw it on one side of a piece of paper. Write your own fishy facts on the other side.

Science Newsroom CD-ROM Choose **Don't Be Dinner** to learn how animals hide.

Recycled Art

Do you think art can be made by only drawing or painting? Think again! Some artists use materials that would be trash.

Try This!

Gather things you no longer need. Think of a sculpture you want to make. Glue the pieces together to create your own recycled art!

Chapter 4 Review

Vocabulary

food web, B42

ocean, B40

pollution, B46

pond, B34

stream, B36

recycle, B49

Use each word once for items 1–6.

1 Many food chains together make up a ____ .

2 When harmful things are in water, air, or land, it is called ____ .

3 A fresh water habitat with moving water is called a ____ .

4 When you save cans so they can be made into new things, you ____ .

5 A fresh water habitat with water that stays in one place is called a ____ .

6 A large body of salt water is called an ____ .

Science Ideas

7 What do pond turtles do for warmth during winter?

8 What do beavers use to make their homes?

Inquiry Skill: Classify

9 Do these plants and animals live in fresh water or salt water? List them in two groups.

crab

frog

lily pad

killer whale

READ
River Home by Susan Blackaby

Did You Ever Wonder? | INQUIRY SKILL | **Investigate** ways you can clean up the land, water, and air.

Melanie Stiassny
MARINE BIOLOGIST

Melanie Stiassny is a marine biologist. She studies oceans. Marine biologists have many questions about life in the oceans. More facts are known about the Moon than about our oceans!

Melanie travels to many places. Sometimes she discovers new kinds of fish, such as the Etia nguti (EE-tee-ah NEW-tee). The female fish keeps her young safe by holding them in her mouth.

Melanie knows that we must care for our oceans. She says we must not take too many fish out of the water. If we do, there may not be any left!

 LOG ON Visit **www.science.mmhschool.com** to learn more about marine biologists and oceans.

TIME FOR KIDS®

This is the jaw of a tiger shark.

Think Big!

Why do you think we know more about the Moon than about our oceans?

Habitat Story

Choose a plant or animal that lives in a land habitat. Write a short story about your plant or animal. What does it need to live in its habitat? How does it get what it needs?

Water Animal Skit

Think of an animal that lives in a water habitat. Pretend you are that animal and act out a story.

For Your Reference

Observe

You **observe** when you use your senses to learn about something. Your senses tell you how things look, sound, feel, smell, or taste.

What you need

pencil

crayons

paper

What to do

1 **Observe** something in the Science Center. How does it look? Feel? Smell? Sound?

2 Draw and write about it.

3 Tell a friend which of your senses helped you the most.

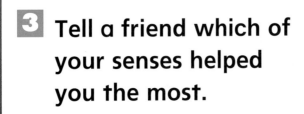

Measure

You can **measure** to find out how long, fast, or warm something is. You use numbers to record the answer.

What to do

1 Fill one cup with warm water. Fill the other cup with cold water.

2 Place a thermometer in each cup. Wait 2 minutes. **Measure** the temperatures.

3 Compare your temperatures with a partner's. Did you both get the same numbers? If not, measure again.

What you need

warm and cold water

2 thermometers

Inquiry Skill Builder 3

Compare

You **compare** things when you show how they are alike and different.

paper

pencil

What to do

1 **Compare** the people.

2 List three ways they are alike. List three ways they are different.

3 Choose an animal. How are the people different from the animal?

R 4

Inquiry Skill Builder 4

Classify

You **classify** when you put things into groups to show how they are alike.

What you need

paper

pencil

What to do

1 Look at the picture of the beans.

2 Classify the beans by size. How many are big? How many are small?

3 Find another way to classify the beans.

Make a Model

You **make a model** when you do something to show a place or thing. A model can help you learn how a place looks or how a thing works.

What to do

1 **Make a model** of a clock. Include numbers and hands.

BE CAREFUL! Scissors are sharp.

2 Tell what you can learn about a real clock from the model.

3 Tell how a real clock is different from the model.

What you need

paper

crayons

scissors

paper fastener

Inquiry Skill Builder 6

Communicate

You **communicate** when you talk, write, or draw to share your ideas.

What to do

1 Think about your favorite food.

2 Write about it and draw a picture.

3 **Communicate** to a friend about your favorite food. Ask your friend to name the food you described.

What you need

paper

pencil

Inquiry Skill Builder 7

Infer

paper

pencil

To **infer**, you use what you know to figure something out.

What to do

1 Look at the pictures. Record what you observe about each picture.

2 Use what you know to **infer** which place is warmer.

3 Write a short story to tell what people do to have fun in each place.

Put Things in Order

To put things **in order**, you tell what happens first, next, and last.

What you need

pencil

crayons

paper

What to do

1 Think about all the things that you did this morning.

2 List the things on your paper. Write them **in order**.

3 Draw a picture of you doing one of those things.

Predict

You **predict** when you use what you know to tell what you think will happen.

"I'm hungry," said Laura.

"Me, too," replied Jack.

"I wish I had a snack," Laura said.

"All I have are these grapes," said Jack.

What you need

crayons

paper

What to do

1 Read the story above.

2 **Predict** what will happen next.

3 Draw a picture to show it.

Inquiry Skill Builder 10

Investigate

When you **investigate**, you make a plan and try it out.

What to do

1 Use clay and pencils to make a shape.

2 How many blocks can your shape hold? **Investigate** to find out. Make a plan and try it.

3 Have a partner try your plan. How many blocks did your partner use? Did you use the same number?

What you need

pencils

clay

blocks

Draw a Conclusion

crayons

To **draw a conclusion**, you use what you observe to explain what happens.

What to do

1 Look at the picture. Where do you think the girl went? What do you think she did?

paper

2 Draw a conclusion. Show it in a picture.

3 Explain your conclusion to a friend. Does your friend agree with you? Why or why not?

Save and Recycle

We should not waste things.

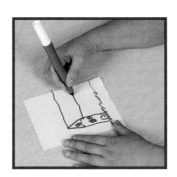

Use no more than you need.

Don't leave the water on.

Recycle as much as you can.

Use things more than once.

Care of Animals

Here are ways to care for animals.

- Give pets food and water. Give them a safe place to live, too.

- Be kind to pets. Handle them with care.

- Don't touch wild animals. They may bite, sting, or scratch you.

- Do not touch things in places where wild animals live.

Care of Plants

Here are ways to care for plants.

- Give plants water and sunlight.

- Ask the teacher before you touch or eat a plant. Some plants can make you very sick!

- Do not dig up plants or pick flowers. Let plants grow where they are.

Clean Up

We need to keep work places clean.

Let an adult clean
up broken glass.

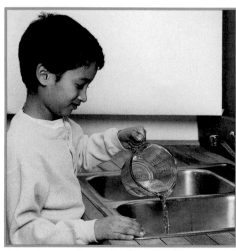

Pour water into a sink,
not into a trash can.

Put food in plastic bags.
This keeps bugs away.

Don't get paint
or food on you.

How to Measure

You can use objects to measure. Line up the objects and count them. Use objects that are alike. They must be the same size.

This string is about 8 paper clips long.

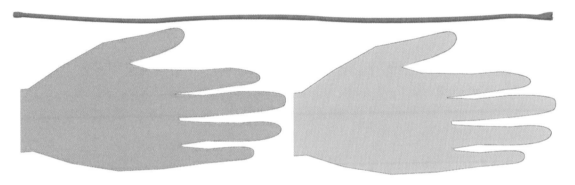

This string is about 2 hands long.

Try This!

● Measure some string. Tell how you did it.

● Can you measure string with these paper clips? Why or why not?

Measure in Centimeters

You can use a ruler to measure. You can use centimeters (cm). This is called a unit of measurement. You can measure this insect. Line up the end of the insect with the 0 on the ruler.

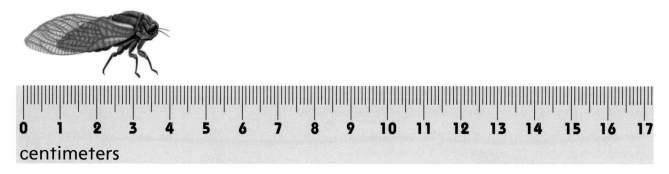

The insect is about 4 centimeters long. We write this as 4 cm.

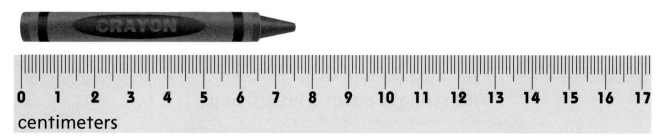

The crayon is about $7\frac{1}{2}$ centimeters long. We write this as $7\frac{1}{2}$ cm.

Try This!

Measure this pencil. Tell how long it is.

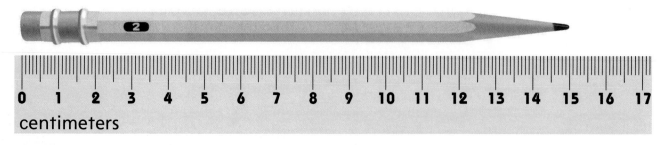

Measure in Inches

You can use inches (in.) to measure, too.
This toy is about $2\frac{1}{2}$ inches, or $2\frac{1}{2}$ in.

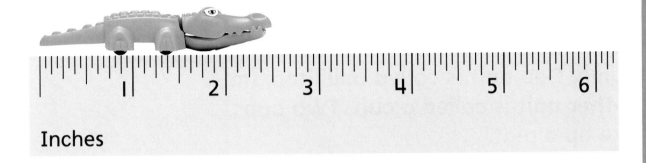

Inches

You can estimate how long something is.
When you estimate, you guess the length.
Then you can use a ruler to measure it.

Try This!

Estimate how long each
object is. Then use a ruler
to measure them.

Object	Estimate	Measure
penny	about ____ in.	____ in.
toy car	about ____ in.	____ in.

Use a Measuring Cup

Volume is the amount of space something takes up. You can use a measuring cup to find volume.

You can use different units to measure volume. One unit is called milliliters (mL). Another unit is called a cup. Two cups make up a pint.

Try This!

- Find a container. Estimate how much water it can hold.

- Then fill it with water. Measure the water in milliliters or cups to find out if you were right.

Use a Balance

A balance compares masses.

Place one object on each side of the balance. The object that has more mass will make that side of the balance go down. The object that has less mass will go up.

Try This!

- Place 2 objects on a balance. Which has more mass?

- Put 3 objects in order from least mass to most mass. Use the balance to check.

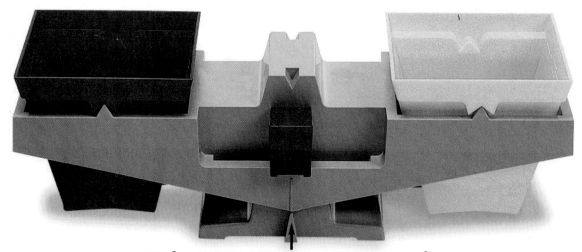

Before you compare masses, make sure the arrow points to the line.

Use a Scale

A scale measures weight. As an animal grows, it gets bigger and gains weight. You can measure weight in pounds (lbs).

Try This!

- What is your weight? First, estimate your weight. Then, use a scale to measure it.

- Every month, measure your weight. Record it in a chart. See how your weight changes as you grow.

Use a Thermometer

A thermometer measures temperature.
There is liquid inside the thermometer.

When it gets warmer, the liquid
moves up.

When it gets cooler, the liquid
moves down.

Which thermometer shows a warmer
temperature? How can you tell?

R 24

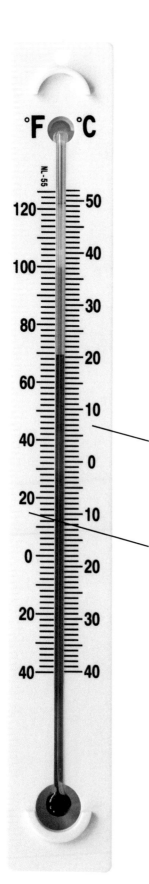

A thermometer measures temperature in degrees. The marks show degrees Fahrenheit and degrees Celsius.

Read this thermometer in degrees Celsius. Look at the numbers on the right side. Find the number where the liquid ends.

degrees
Celsius

degrees
Fahrenheit

Try This!

Read the thermometers on page R24. What temperatures are shown?

Use Weather Tools

You can use weather tools to measure the weather. A thermometer tells you how hot or cool the air is outside.

A rain gauge tells you how much rain falls. It has a jar that catches the rain. It also has a ruler to measure how much rain falls into the jar.

weather vane

rain gauge

wind sock

A wind sock and weather vane tell which way the wind blows. The arrow on a weather vane tells where the wind is coming from. It points to the north, south, east, or west.

An anemometer measures how fast the wind blows. It tells you the wind's speed.

Try This!

Use a rain gauge. Measure how much rain falls on two different days that rain. Compare the amounts.

anemometer

Use a Clock

A clock measures time.

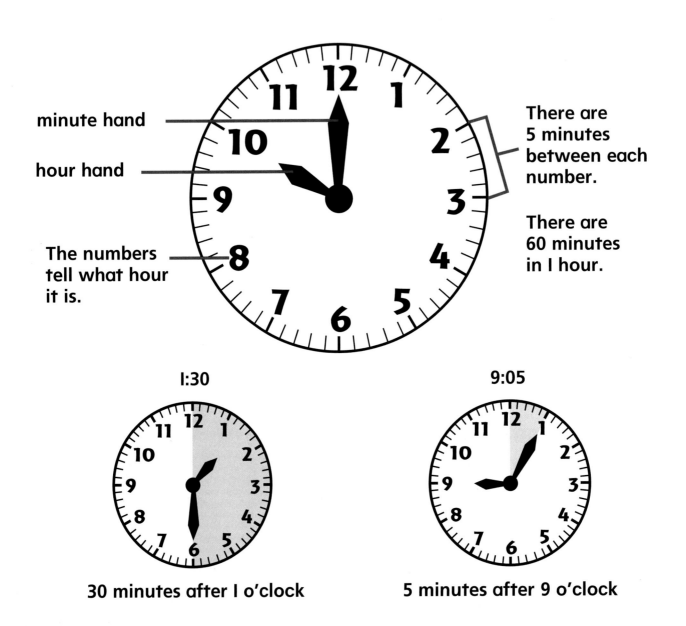

minute hand

hour hand

The numbers tell what hour it is.

There are 5 minutes between each number.

There are 60 minutes in 1 hour.

1:30

30 minutes after 1 o'clock

9:05

5 minutes after 9 o'clock

Try This!

Estimate how long you sleep each night.
Use a clock to find out.

Use a Hand Lens

A hand lens makes objects seem larger.

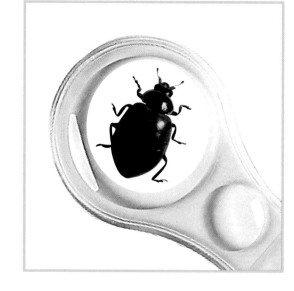

First, move the lens away from the object. Stop when the object looks fuzzy.

Next, move the lens a little closer to the object. Stop when the object looks clear.

Try This!

● Observe each bug here. Use a hand lens.

● How many legs do you see on the bugs?

● What else can you see?

R 29

Use a Computer

You can use a computer to get information.

You can use CD-ROMs. They save a lot of information. You can fit many books on one CD-ROM!

You can also use the Internet. The Internet links your computer to ones far away.

Try This!

Visit **www.science.mmhschool.com** to find out more about science in your world.

Your Body

Each part of your body has a job to do.

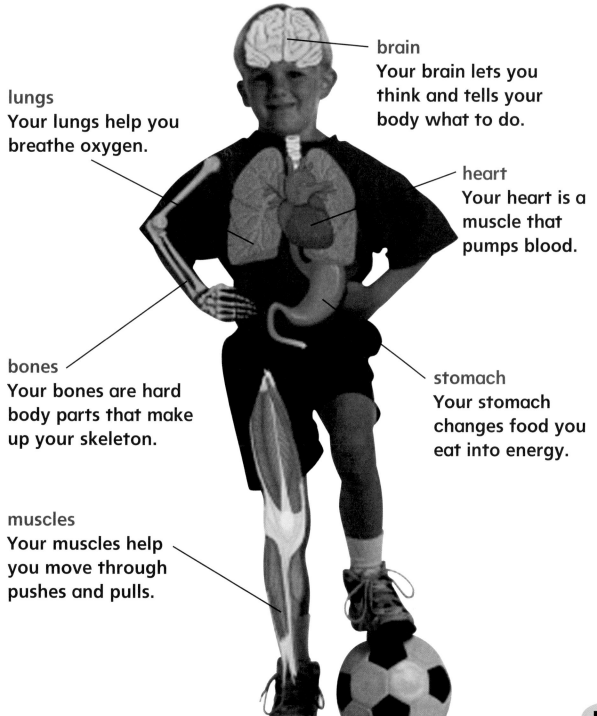

lungs
Your lungs help you breathe oxygen.

brain
Your brain lets you think and tells your body what to do.

heart
Your heart is a muscle that pumps blood.

bones
Your bones are hard body parts that make up your skeleton.

stomach
Your stomach changes food you eat into energy.

muscles
Your muscles help you move through pushes and pulls.

R 31

Take Care of Your Body

Keep your body clean.

Brush and floss your teeth.

Take care of your hair and nails.

Sit and stand up tall.

Wash your hands before and after you eat.

Germs are on things you touch.
Germs can make you sick.

Wash your hands often.

Eat Healthful Foods

Healthful foods give your body energy. You use energy to walk, play, and move. You need energy to help you grow and stay healthy.

Choose healthful foods.

Milk helps your teeth and bones grow.

Fruits and vegetables give you energy.
Bread and cereal do, too.

Meat helps your muscles grow.

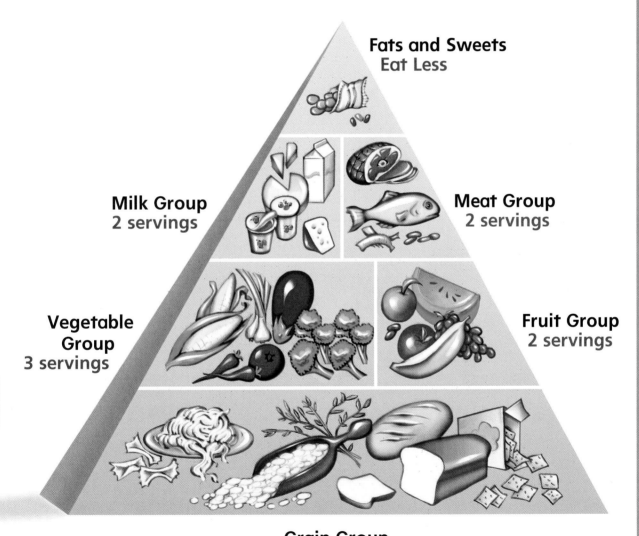

Fats and Sweets
Eat Less

Milk Group
2 servings

Meat Group
2 servings

**Vegetable
Group**
3 servings

Fruit Group
2 servings

Grain Group
6 servings

Be Active and Rest

Be active every day.
When you are active,
your heart beats faster.
This keeps you healthy
and strong.

Get plenty of
sleep at night.

These things
help you grow!

Stay Healthy

Your body grows and changes.

Get checkups every year.

Doctors and dentists can help you stay healthy as you grow. They can help you get better when you are sick.

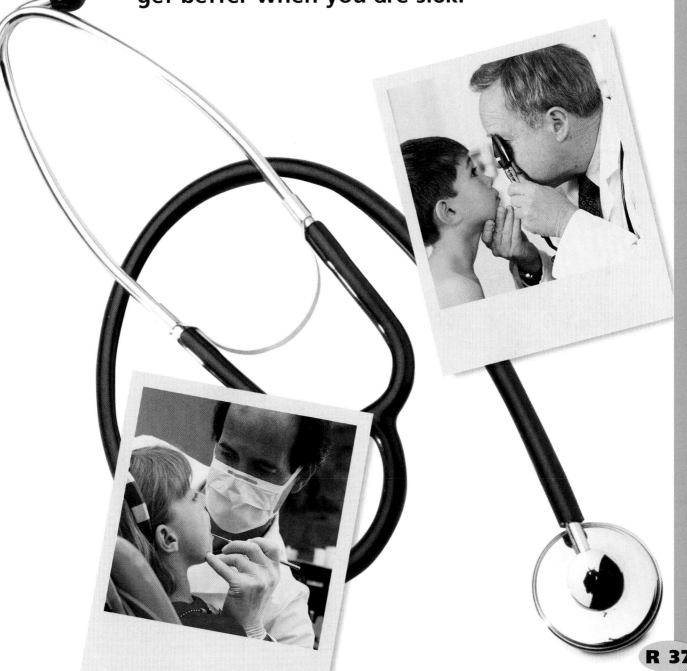

Be Safe Indoors

Some things are dangerous. Don't touch them!
Tell an adult when you find something dangerous.

Be Safe Outdoors

Follow safety rules.

Wear a helmet.

Buckle up!

STOP

Cross at the corner.

Play safely.

Getting Along

Work and play well with others.

Respect one another's feelings.

Show others that you care.

Glossary

A

amphibians animals that start their lives in the water *(page A35)* **Frogs and toads are amphibians.**

Arctic a very cold place near the North Pole *(page B24)* **In the Arctic, snow is on the ground for much of the year.**

attract to pull *(page F38)* **A magnet can attract some metals.**

axis a line through the center of a spinning object *(page D6)* **Earth's axis is an imaginary line that goes from the North Pole to the South Pole.**

axis

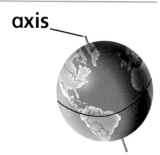

C

chemical change when matter changes into different matter *(page E22)* **When metal rusts, a chemical change happens.**

classify to put things into groups to show how they are alike *(page A4)* **You can classify animals by their legs.**

legs

no legs

LOG **Visit www.science.mmhschool.com**
ON to find out more about these words.

communicate to share your ideas with others *(page A36)* **Scientists communicate to learn and to show what they know.**

compare to tell how things are alike and different *(page D10)* **You can compare how the balls are alike and different. One is blue, and the other is red.**

compass a tool with a magnetic needle that always points to Earth's North Pole *(page F49)* **With a compass, you can figure out which direction you are facing.**

condense to change from a gas to a liquid *(page C7)* **Cool air makes water vapor condense.**

constellation a star pattern that makes a picture *(page D40)* **The Big Dipper and the Little Dipper are constellations.**

craters large holes on the surface of the Moon *(page D27)* **Many Moon craters were made by rocks falling from space.**

D

desert a dry habitat that gets very little rainfall *(page B20)* **A desert gets less than ten inches of rain each year.**

draw a conclusion to use what you observe to explain what happens *(page B18)* **You can draw a conclusion about what kind of weather is shown here.**

E

earthquake a shaking of the ground caused by a shift of Earth's crust *(page C20)* **An earthquake causes Earth to change.**

endangered in danger of becoming extinct *(page C48)* **The giant panda is an endangered animal.**

energy what makes matter move or change *(page E32)* **Fireworks give off energy.**

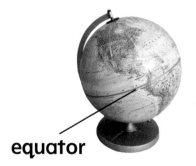

equator the imaginary line around the middle of Earth that separates the northern part from the southern part *(page D16)* **The United States is north of the equator.**

equator

erosion when worn down rocks are carried away *(page C14)* **Erosion caused the Grand Canyon to form.**

evaporate to change from a liquid to a gas *(page C6)* **The boy's sweatshirt dries because the water evaporates.**

extinct when a living thing dies out and no more of its kind are living anywhere on Earth *(page C46)* **The woolly mammoth is extinct.**

F

flower the part of a plant that makes seeds *(page A12)* **Seeds grow inside the flower.**

food chain the order in which energy moves from one living thing to another *(page A41)* **In a food chain, each animal uses another living thing as food.**

food web a group of several food chains that are connected *(page B42)* **Plankton is an important part of the ocean food web.**

force a push or a pull that makes something move or change direction *(page F6)* **The girl moves forward with the help of a force.**

fossils what is left of living things from the past *(page C32)* **Some fossils are animal footprints.**

friction a force that slows down moving things *(page F12)* **A skater stops by using friction.**

fruit the part of a plant that grows around seeds *(page A13)* **The fruit protects the seeds.**

fuel something that gives off heat when it burns *(page E34)* **Wood, natural gas, and oil are fuels.**

fulcrum the fixed point on which a lever rests *(page F21)* **A seesaw rests on a fulcrum.**

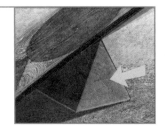

G

gas a state of matter that spreads out to fill its container *(page E16)* **A balloon is filled with gas.**

gravity a force that pulls things toward Earth *(page F7)* **Gravity pulls the sled down the hill.**

H

habitat a place where plants and animals can meet their needs *(page B6)* **This goat lives in a mountain habitat.**

heat a kind of energy that can change matter's state *(page E32)* **Heat can change a solid to a liquid.**

I

infer to use what you know to figure something out *(page A14)* **You can infer what kind of animal made these footprints.**

investigate to make a plan and try it out *(page E18)* **You can investigate how to make a magnet attract a paper clip through water.**

L

landslide a sudden movement of soil down a hill *(page C21)* **A landslide can destroy homes.**

larva the stage in the life cycle of a butterfly when the insect is a caterpillar *(page A48)* **A caterpillar is a larva.**

lever a simple machine made of a bar that rests on a fixed point *(page F21)* **You can make a lever with two pencils.**

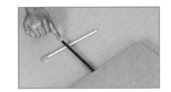

life cycle shows how a living thing grows, lives, and dies *(page A18)* **A bear's life cycle shows how a bear grows.**

light a kind of energy that lets us see *(page E38)* **We use light from lamps to help us see indoors.**

liquid a state of matter that takes the shape of its container *(page E14)* **Juice is a liquid.**

M

magnetic field the area around a magnet where its force pulls *(page F42)* **A magnetic field can pull through solids, liquids, and gases.**

make a model to make something to show a place or thing *(page B8)* **You can make a model to show where leaf bats live.**

mammals animals with hair or fur that breathe with body parts called lungs *(page A34)* **Female mammals make milk for their babies.**

mass the amount of matter in an object *(page E7)* **A feather has less mass than a crayon.**

matter anything that takes up space and has mass *(page E6)* **Everything in this fish tank is made of matter.**

measure to find out how long, how much, or how warm something is *(page F4)* **You can use a ruler to measure items.**

migrate to move to another place *(page B13)* **In winter these animals migrate to a warmer habitat.**

minerals parts of rock and soil that plants and animals need *(page A7)* **A tree uses minerals in the soil to stay healthy.**

Moon a ball of rock that orbits around Earth *(page D26)* **It takes the Moon about 27 days to finish its orbit around Earth.**

observe to use your senses to learn about the world around you *(page B38)* **Scientists observe things to learn more about them.**

ocean a large, deep body of salt water *(page B40)* **Dolphins live in the ocean.**

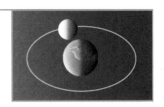

orbit the path something takes as it moves around an object *(page D12)* **The Moon moves around Earth in an orbit.**

order to show what happens first, second, third, and last *(page A44)* **When you put things in order you can tell what will happen next.**

oxygen a gas found in the air we breathe *(page A23)* **A whale needs to breathe oxygen to live.**

P

paleontologist a scientist who studies things that lived long ago *(page C38)* **A paleontologist finds and studies fossils.**

phase the Moon's shape that we can see from Earth *(page D32)* **We see phases of the Moon because we see different parts of its lit side.**

physical change to change the size or shape of matter *(page E20)* **When you cut food, a physical change happens.**

pitch how high or how low a sound is (*page E47*) **You can play a high pitch or a low pitch on a xylophone.**

planet a huge object that travels around the Sun (*page D44*) **Saturn is a planet in our solar system.**

poles the ends of a magnet where the pull is strongest (*page F40*) **Every magnet has two poles.**

pollen the powder inside a flower that can make seeds grow (*page A16*) **The bee carries the pollen from flower to flower.**

pollution the effect of harmful things in water, air, or land (*page B46*) **Pollution hurts living things.**

pond a fresh water habitat in which the water stays in one place (*page B34*) **Beavers build their homes in a pond.**

precipitation water falling from the sky as rain, snow, and hail (*page C9*) **Rain is a kind of precipitation.**

predator an animal that hunts another animal for food (*page A40*) **Sharks are predators.**

predict to use what you know to tell what you think will happen *(page A10)* **You can predict what might grow from these seeds.**

prey an animal that is hunted *(page A40)* **The bird is the cat's prey.**

property something that tells you about an object *(page E8)* **Big, brown, and fuzzy are all properties of this bear.**

pupa the stage in the life cycle of a butterfly when a caterpillar makes a hard case around itself *(page A48)* **Inside the hard case, the pupa changes into a butterfly.**

R

rain forest a habitat where it rains almost every day *(page B16)* **A rain forest can get more than 70 inches of rain each year.**

ramp a simple machine with a slanted surface *(page F26)* **A ramp makes it easier to move from place to place.**

recycle to use waste to make new things that can be used again *(page B49)* **We can recycle paper, glass, cans, and plastic.**

reflect to bounce off an object *(page E38)* **A mirror reflects light.**

refraction when light bends as it passes through something *(page E39)* **Refraction can make something look bigger.**

repel to push away from *(page F41)* **The poles of these magnets repel each other.**

reptiles animals with scaly skin *(page A34)* **Snakes are reptiles.**

rotate to spin *(page D6)* **Earth rotates on its axis.**

rotates —

S

seeds the plant parts that can grow into new plants *(page A13)* **Seeds begin to grow when they get water, warmth, and air.**

shelter a place where an animal can live and be safe *(page A42)* **Foxes find shelter in a hole.**

simple machine something that helps you lift or move an object *(page F20)* **A ramp is a simple machine.**

skeleton a full set of bones *(page C39)* **A dinosaur skeleton helps scientists learn what dinosaurs looked like.**

solar system the Sun, nine planets, and all of their moons *(page D44)* **The Sun is the center of our solar system.**

solid a state of matter that has a shape of its own *(page E12)* **This wooden block is a solid.**

sound a kind of energy that you hear *(page E44)* **When you crash cymbals together, they make a loud sound.**

star a hot ball in the sky that makes its own light *(page D38)* **A star looks tiny because it is so far away from Earth.**

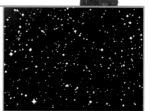

stream a fresh water habitat with moving water *(page B36)* **Plants and animals live in and around a stream.**

Sun the closest star to Earth *(page D7)* **The Sun gives Earth heat and light.**

T

temperature how warm something is
(page E9) **You can measure temperature
by using a thermometer.**

V

vibrate to move back and forth *(page E44)*
**When a string vibrates, you can hear
sound.**

volcano a mountain formed when hot,
melted rock builds up and bursts through
the surface of Earth *(page C22)* **Mt. St. Helens
is a volcano that erupted in 1980.**

volume the amount of space that a thing
takes up *(page E15)* **You can measure the
volume of a liquid with measuring cups.**

W

water cycle the movement of water
between the ground and sky *(page C8)* **Rain
and snow are parts of the water cycle.**

water vapor water that has become a gas
(page C6) **When water boils, some of the
water turns into water vapor.**

woodland forest a habitat that gets
enough rain and sunlight for trees to
grow well *(page B10)* **Many plants and
animals live in a woodland forest.**

Credits

Cover Photos: c. Joe McDonald/McDonald Wildlife Photography; bkgd. Daryl Benson/Masterfile; spine Joe McDonald/McDonald Wildlife Photography; Back Cover: bkgd. Daryl Benson/Masterfile; t.l. Frank Fournier/Contact Press Images; t.r. Tim Parsley/Index Stock Imagery; c.l. John Lamb/Stone/Getty Images; c.r. Frank Zullo/Photo Researchers, Inc.; b.l. Donovan Reese/Stone/Getty Images; b.r. Karl Weatherly/Stone/Getty Images. Endpaper: Daryl Benson/Masterfile

Photography Credits: All photos are by Macmillan/McGraw-Hill (MMH) and Dave Mager for MMH, Ray Boudreau for MMH, Michael Groen for MMH, Ken Karp for MMH, Ron Tanaka for MMH, and David Waitz for MMH except as noted below:

i: bkgd. Daryl Benson/Masterfile; t.l. Zefa Visual Media-Germany/Index Stock Imagery; b.l. D. Cox/OSF/Animals Animals. iii: Robert Franz/Index Stock Imagery. iv: bkgd. Taxi/Getty Images; t. NASA/CORBIS; c., b. Courtesy, Sally Ride. v: l. Siede Preis/PhotoDisc/Getty Images; r. Jeff L. Lepore/Photo Researchers, Inc. vi: l. Keren Su/Stock Boston; b. Paul Zahl/Photo Researchers, Inc. vii: l. Tim Parsley/Index Stock Imagery; r. Leonard Lee Rue/Stock Boston. viii: l. John Lamb/Stone/Getty Images; b. Bob Burch/Bruce Coleman, Inc. ix: l. Frank Zullo/Photo Researchers Inc; b. NASA/Science Force/Photo Researchers, Inc. x: l. Donovan Reese/Stone/Getty Images; b. Bill Gallery/Stock Boston. xi: l. Karl Weatherly/Stone/Getty Images; b. Will Ryan/The Stock Market/CORBIS. xv: t.l., t.r. PhotoDisc/Getty Images. xvi: t.c., c., c.l. PhotoDisc/Getty Images; b.l. Siede Preis/PhotoDisc/Getty Images. SO: Susan Rosenthal/CORBIS. S0-S1: Michael & Patricia Fogden/CORBIS. S2: David Young-Wolff/PhotoEdit. S3: Jeff L. Lepore/Photo Researchers, Inc. S4-S5: F. Sieb/ Robertstock.com. S6: C Squared Studios/PhotoDisc/Getty Images; S7: Siede Preis/PhotoDisc/Getty Images. S8-S9: Burke/Triolo Productions/Brand X Pictures. S10-S11: Marc Romanelli/Getty Images. S12: David Young-Wolff/PhotoEdit. S13: bkgd. Artbase Inc.; l. Michael Ederegger/DRK Photo; t.r. D. Suzio/Photo Researchers, Inc.; c.r. Gary Moszaros/Photo Researchers, Inc.; b.r. Burke/Triolo Productions/Brand X Pictures. S14-S15: Royalty-Free/CORBIS/MAGMA. S16: l. David H. Wells/CORBIS. AO: Frank Fournier/Contact Press Images. A0-A1: Keren Su/Stock Boston. A1: Frank Fournier/Contact Press Images. A2-A3: John Gerlach/DRK Photo. A4-A5: Jeanne White/Photo Researchers, Inc. A6: l. Tom Bean/DRK Photo; l. inset Aaron Haupt/Stock Boston; r. inset E.R. Degginger/Color-Pic, Inc. A6-A7: sky John Eastcott/DRK Photo; soil Susanna Price/DK Images; c. E.R. Degginger/Color-Pic, Inc. A7: l. Siede Preis/PhotoDisc/PictureQuest; r. Ross Durant/FoodPix. A8: Christian Grzimek/Photo Researchers, Inc. A8-A9: HOLT Studios/Photo Researchers, Inc. A9: r. Patti Murray/Earth Scenes; l. Alan & Linda Detrick/Photo Researchers, Inc. A10-A11: John Kaprielian/Photo Researchers, Inc. A12: flowers and plant Leslye Borden/PhotoEdit; tomatoes Mary Kate Denny/PhotoEdit. A12-A13: soil Susanna Price/DK Images. A13: l. Johnny's Selected Seeds; r. David/Jules Murray/Selmes/DK Images. A14-A15: Richard Hutchings/PhotoEdit. A15: t.r. PhotoDisc/Getty Images; t.c.r. Spencer Grant/PhotoEdit. A16: l. Patti Murray/Earth Scenes; r. Patricia Agre/ Photo Researchers, Inc.; bee M.P.L. Fogden/Bruce Coleman, Inc. A17: t. Michael Newman/PhotoEdit; b.l. Jerry Howard/Stock Boston; r. Felicia Martinez/PhotoEdit. A18: b.l. Leonard Lessin/Peter Arnold, Inc.; b.c. Alfred B. Thomas/Earth Scenes; roots Dwight Kuhn Photography. A18-A19: t. John Kaprielian/Photo Researchers, Inc.; b. Susanna Price/DK Images. A19: Patti Murray/Earth Scenes. A20-A21: Tom Salyer/Silver Image for MMH. A22: t.l. David Young-Wolff/PhotoEdit; inset Aaron Haupt/Stock Boston; b.l. RDF/Visuals Unlimited; b.r. Alan & Linda Detrick/Photo Researchers, Inc. A22-A23: Richard Shiell/Earth Scenes. A23: t.l. Russell Lincoln/ Stock Boston; t.r. Myrleen Cate/PhotoEdit; b.l. RDF/Visuals Unlimited. A24: l. Maximillian Stock Ltd./Earth Scenes. A26: C.C. Lockwood/Bruce Coleman Inc. A30-A31: Douglas Faulkner/Photo Researchers, Inc. A32: t. Donald Specker/ Animals Animals; b. John Cancalosi/Stock Boston. A32-A33: bkgd. Tom Brakefield/DRK Photo. A33: t.l. Jim Brandenburg/Minden Pictures; b.l. Tim Rock/Animals Animals; c.l. Frans Lanting/Minden Pictures; c.r. Konrad Wothe/Minden Pictures; t.r. Lisa Husar/DRK Photo; b.r. Allen Blake Sheldon/ Animals Animals. A34: t. Breck Kent/Animals Animals; c. Wayne Lynch/DRK Photo; b. Anup Shah/DRK Photo. A35: t. Russell C. Hansen/Peter Arnold, Inc.; c. Paul Zahl/Photo Researchers, Inc.; b. Patrice Ceisel/Stock Boston. A36-A37: Rafi Bewn-Shahar/DRK Photo. A38-A39: Carl Sams/Peter Arnold, Inc. A39: r. Johnny Johnson/DRK Photo; b. Mitsuaki Iwago/Minden Pictures. A40: t. James Watt/ Animals Animals; b.l. Laura Riley/Bruce Coleman, Inc.; b.r. John Gerlach/DRK Photo. A41: t.r. John Kaprielian/Photo Researchers, Inc.; inset D. Cavagnaro/Peter Arnold, Inc.; l. Walter E. Harvay/Photo Researchers, Inc.; b. Jane Burton/Bruce Coleman, Inc. A42: b. Paul Berquist/Animals Animals. A42-A43: Frans Lanting/ Minden Pictures. A43: l. C. Allan Morgan/Peter Arnold, Inc.; r. Olen S. Hansen/ Photo Researchers, Inc. A44-A45: Margot Conte/Animals Animals. A46: Wayne Lynch/DRK Photo. A46-A47: Lisa & Mike Husar/DRK Photo. A47: t. Stephen J. Krasemann/DRK Photo; b. Tom & Pat Leeson/DRK Photo. A48: Kim Taylor/DK Images. A48-A49: John Eastcott/DRK Photo. A49: Kim Taylor/DK Images. A51: t. Rod Planck/Photo Researchers, Inc.; c. Norbert Wu/Minden Pictures; b. D. Cavagnaro/DRK Photo. A53: t. Anup Shah/DRK Photo; b. Kim Taylor/DK Images. A54-A55: Dan Helms/National Geographic Image Collection. A56: b. Jane Burton/Bruce Coleman, Inc. BO: Tim Parsley/Index Stock Imagery. B0-B1: bkgd. Reinhard Eisele/CORBIS; inset PhotoDisc/Getty Images. B2-B3: Claudia Adams/ Dembinsky Photo Associates. B4-B5: Tom Walker/Stock Boston. B5: b. Lynda Richardson/CORBIS. B6: l. George Bernard/Animals Animals; r. M.C. Chamberlain/ DRK Photo. B6-B7: William Johnson/Stock Boston. B7: t. Fritz Polking/Dembinsky Photo Associates; b. E.R. Degginger/Dembinsky Photo Associates. B8-B9: David Ulmer/Stock Boston. B10: l. DPA/Dembinsky Photo Associates; r. Robert Ginn/ PhotoEdit. B10-B11: Owen Franken/Stock Boston. B11: l. Clouds Hill Imaging Ltd./CORBIS; b. Joe McDonald/Animals Animals; r. Tom & Pat Leeson/DRK Photo. B12: t. Terry Donnelly/Dembinsky Photo Associates; c. Skip Moody/Dembinsky Photo Associates; b.l. DPA/Dembinsky Photo Associates; b.r. Anthony Mercieca/ Dembinsky Photo Associates. B13: t. Barbara Gerlach/Dembinsky Photo Associates; t.c. Mark Newman/Bruce Coleman, Inc.; b.c. Breck P. Kent/Animals Animals; b. Adam Jones/Dembinsky Photo Associates. B14: Michael Fogden/DRK Photo. B14-B15: Thomas Fletcher/Stock Boston. B16: Kevin & Suzette Hanley/Animals Animals. B16-B17: Tom & Pat Leeson/DRK Photo. B17: l. Richard La Val/Animals Animals; r. G.W. Willis/Animals Animals. B18-B19: Adam Jones/Dembinsky Photo Associates. B20: l. Jon Gerlach/DRK Photo; b. E.R. Degginger/Dembinsky Photo Associates. B20-B21: Joe McDonald/Earth Scenes. B21: C. Allan Morgan/DRK Photo. B22: Johnny Johnson/DRK Photo. B22-B23: Tom Walker/Stock Boston. B24: l. Eastcott/Momatiuk/Earth Scenes; b. Matthew Neil McVay/Stock Boston. B24-B25: Leonard Lee Rue III/Animals Animals. B25: t. Phyllis Greenberg/Animals Animals; b. Mark J. Thomas/Dembinsky Photo Associates. B26: t.l. Terry Donnelly/Dembinsky Photo Associates; t.r. Joe McDonald/Earth Scenes; c. Hans Strand/Stone/Getty Images; b. Thomas Fletcher/Stock Boston. B29: t.l. E.R. Degginger/Dembinsky Photo Associates; t.c. David Ulmer/Stock Boston; t.r. C. Allan Morgan/DRK Photo; b.r. Tom Walker/Stock Boston. B30-B31: bkgd. Pat & Tom Leeson/Photo Researchers, Inc. B32-B33: S. Nielsen/DRK Photo. B34: t. George Godfrey/Earth Scenes; b. Jim Battles/Dembinsky Photo Associates. B34-B35: Joe McDonald/ Animals Animals. B35: t.l. Rod Planck/Dembinsky Photo Associates; t.r. Johnny Johnson/Animals Animals; b. John Mitchell/Photo Researchers, Inc. B36: t. K. Ringland/Animals Animals; b. Jim Roetzel/Dembinsky Photo Associates. B36-B37: Willard Clay/Dembinsky Photo Associates. B37: l. Hans Reinhard/Bruce Coleman, Inc.; r. Leonard Lee Rue/Stock Boston. B38-B39: Jeff Foott/DRK Photo. B40: l. Susan Blanchet/Dembinsky Photo Associates; r. Reinhard Dirscherl/Alamy. B40-B41: bkgd. Villoch-V&W/Bruce Coleman, Inc.; t. Doug Perrine/DRK Photo. B41: t. Chuck Place/Stock Boston; b.l. D.P. Wilson/Dembinsky Photo Associates; b.r. P. Parks/ Animals Animals. B42: b.l. E.R. Degginger/Earth Scenes; b.r. Norbert Wu/DRK Photo; c. P. Parks/Animals Animals. B42-B43: bkgd. John Gerlach/Earth Scenes; t. Kim Heacox/DRK Photo; b. Jack Grove/PhotoEdit. B43: Jeffry Myers/Stock Boston. B44-B45: M. Harvey/DRK Photo. B46: t. Thomas R. Fletcher/Stock Boston; b. M. Harvey/DRK Photo. B47: t. A. Ramey/Stock Boston; b. Michael Newman/PhotoEdit. B48: t. Lawrence Migdale/Stock Boston; b. Donald Dietz/Stock Boston. B49: t. Zig Leszczynski/Earth Scenes; b. Julie Houck/Stock Boston. B51: t. Group III Kerr/Bruce Coleman, Inc. B53: t.l. George H.H. Huey/Animals Animals; t.r., c.l. Jim Battles/ Dembinsky Photo Associates; c.r. Jeffry Myers/Stock Boston. B54: American Museum of Natural History. B54-B55: c. Denis Finnin/American Museum of Natural History; bkgd. Villoch-V&W/Bruce Coleman, Inc. CO: John Lamb/Stone/Getty Images. C0-C1: James Randklev/Stone/Getty Images. C2-C3: Larry Miller/Photo Researchers, Inc. C4-C5: David Young-Wolff/PhotoEdit. C6: Jon Serafin for MMH. C7: l. Jon Serafin for MMH; r. Scott Smith/Animals Animals. C10: t. Adam Jones/Dembinsky Photo Associates; b. Don Smetzer/PhotoEdit. C10-C11: D. Lloyd/Weatherstock. C11: Warren Faidley/Weatherstock. C12-C13: David A. Bast/Photo Researchers, Inc. C14-C15: Dick Canby/DRK Photo. C15: t. Bob Burch/Bruce Coleman, Inc.; b. Terry Donnelly/Dembinsky Photo Associates. C16-C17: t. Tom Bean/DRK Photo; b. M.H. Black/Bruce Coleman, Inc. C17: David Woodfall/DRK Photo. C18-C19: Tom McHugh/Photo Researchers, Inc. C20: Norman O. Tomalin/Bruce Coleman, Inc. C20-C21: Tom McHugh/Photo Researchers, Inc. C22: Pat & Tom Leeson/Photo Researchers, Inc. C22-C23: David Weintraub/Photo Researchers, Inc. C23: t. David Weintraub/Photo Researchers, Inc.; b. Michael P. Gadomski/Earth Scenes. C24: t.l. Comstock Images/Alamy. C27: t.l. Don Smetzer/ PhotoEdit; t.r. Adam Jones/Dembinsky Photo Associates; b.r. Terry Donnelly/ Dembinsky Photo Associates. C28-C29: Sinclair Stammers/Photo Researchers, Inc. C30-C31: T.A. Wiewandt/DRK Photo. C32: t. Francois Gohier/Photo Researchers, Inc.; l. Joy Spurr/Bruce Coleman, Inc.; b. Dr. David R. Schwimmer/Bruce Coleman, Inc. C32-C33: J.C. Carton/Bruce Coleman, Inc. C33: t. Sinclair Stammers/Photo Researchers, Inc.; b. Tom McHugh & Natural History Museum of L.A. County/Photo Researchers, Inc. C35: David Schwimmer/Bruce Coleman, Inc. C36-C37: Bob Burch/Bruce Coleman, Inc. C38: Pete Larson/Black Hills Institute. C38-C39: Ira Block/National Geographic Image Collection. C39: Ira Block/National Geographic Image Collection. C40: t. Bob Burch/Bruce Coleman, Inc.; b. Michael Fogden/ Animals Animals. C41: t.l. Claudia Adams/Dembinsky Photo Associates; t.r. Stephen J. Krasemann/DRK Photo; b.l. Francois Gohier/Photo Researchers, Inc.; b.r. Stan Osolinski/Dembinsky Photo Associates. C44-C45: Tom & Pat Leeson/DRK Photo. C46: t. Don & Pat Valenti/DRK Photo; b. Stephen J. Krasemann/DRK Photo. C46-C47: Francois Gohier/Photo Researchers, Inc. C47: t. George Bernard/Animals Animals; b. Michael Fogden/Bruce Coleman, Inc. C48: t. Maresa Pryor/Earth Scenes; t.c. Henry Ausloos/Animals Animals; b.c. Alan D. Carey/Photo Researchers, Inc.; b.l. Pat & Rae Hagan/Bruce Coleman, Inc. C48-C49: David N. Davis/Photo Researchers, Inc. C49: t. Erwin & Peggy Bauer/Bruce Coleman, Inc.; b. Bruce M. Herman/Photo Researchers, Inc. C52: t. Bob Burch/Bruce Coleman, Inc.; b. Michael Fogden/ Animals Animals. C53: t. Francois Gohier/Photo Researchers, Inc. C54: O. Louis Mazzatenta/National Geographic Image Collection. C54-C55: O. Louis Mazzatenta/ National Geographic Image Collection. C55: CORBIS. DO: Frank Zullo/Photo Researchers, Inc. D0-D1: Science Photo Library/Photo Researchers, Inc. D2-D3: NASA. D4: Rafael Macia/Photo Researchers, Inc. D4-D5: Rafael Macia/Photo Researchers, Inc. D6: Jonathan Nourok/PhotoEdit. D6-D7: Byron Jorjorian/Bruce Coleman, Inc. D7: Jisas/Lockheed/Science Photo Library/Photo Researchers, Inc. D10: Don & Pat Valenti/DRK Photo. D10-D11: Robert Aschenbrenner/Stock Boston. D14-D15: Dennis Flaherty/Photo Researchers, Inc. D16: t. James Blank/Bruce Coleman, Inc.; b. Antipodes/Gamma Sport. D17: Jacques Jangoux/Photo Researchers, Inc. D20: Jacques Jangoux/Photo Researchers, Inc. D22-D23: BMDO/NRL/LLNL/Science Photo Library/Photo Researchers, Inc. D24: t. David Nunuk/Photo Researchers, Inc.; b. Bruce Coleman, Inc. D24-D25: John W. Bova/Photo Researchers, Inc. D26-D27: David Nunuk/Photo Researchers, Inc. D28: moon David Nunuk/Photo Researchers, Inc. D28-D29: t. Images Colour Library/ Natural Selection; b. Novastock/Photo Researchers, Inc. D29: t. David Nunuk/Photo Researchers, Inc. D30: John Sanford/Science Photo Library/Photo Researchers, Inc. D30-D31: Larry Landolfi/Photo Researchers, Inc. D32: John Sanford/Science Photo Library/Photo Researchers, Inc. D33: l. John W. Bova/Photo Researchers, Inc.; c., r. John Sanford/Science Photo Library/Photo Researchers, Inc. D34: l., c. John Sanford/Science Photo Library/Photo Researchers, Inc.; r. John Bova/Photo Researchers, Inc. D35: John Sanford/Science Photo Library/Photo Researchers, Inc. D36-D37: John Foster/Photo Researchers, Inc. D38: inset David Parker/Photo Researchers, Inc.; b.l. Dr. E.I. Robson/Photo Researchers, Inc. D38-D39: Allan